You Can
Be Happy

IN SPITE OF EVERYTHING

You
CAN
Be Happy
IN SPITE OF EVERYTHING

Paramhansa Yogananda

CRYSTAL CLARITY PUBLISHERS
Nevada City, California

© 2025 by Hansa Trust

All rights reserved. Published 2025

Printed in the United States of America

Crystal Clarity Publishers

crystalclarity.com | clarity@crystalclarity.com

14618 Tyler Foote Rd. | Nevada City, California

800.424.1055

ISBN 978-1-56589-250-7 (print) | LCCN 2025021267

ISBN 978-1-56589-647-5 (e-book) | LCCN 2025021268

ISBN 978-1-56589-850-9 (audiobook)

Cover design by Tejindra Scott Tully

Interior layout and design by Michele Madhavi Molloy

Contents

Publisher's Note

Dear Reader,

Welcome to the first edition of our new "Seeds of Light" series, which consists of inspiring articles written by the great spiritual Master, Paramhansa Yogananda.

In 1920, he left India, traveling to a foreign culture, America, to spread the ancient wisdom of Self-realization. Nobody at that time knew anything about yogic science, and he had to start from zero, which was undoubtedly a daunting task.

However, Yogananda swept the West with his highly successful lecture tours ("campaigns," as he called them). The yogic message spread everywhere. That is why he is often called "the father of yoga in the West" today.

After five years, in 1925, he started publishing his magazine, "East-West," later "Inner Culture." As one reads on its cover, it was dedicated to

"Spiritual realization; development of body, mind, and soul; practical metaphysics; and Hindu psychology."

In these magazines, Yogananda offered his enlightened message in short and long articles on all sorts of topics. The book you are reading contains a selection of these articles: those in which the Master focused on happiness, which is both a creative art and a concrete science, and it can be felt despite all our life difficulties. The art, for example, is this: "Happiness comes, not by helplessly wishing for it, but by dreaming, thinking, and living it in all the moods and actions of life."

You are reading unedited, authentic, pure material from these precious early magazines. It is as if the young Yogananda were talking directly to you, without any filter.

Enjoy the gift of Yogananda's luminous teachings, which are truly "Seeds of Light."

With Love,
Crystal Clarity Publishers

Acquiring Happiness

We can never be happy unless we are progressing and seeking satisfaction in doing so, and unless we are guarding our happiness from all the influences which destroy it.

Happiness comes, not by helplessly thinking, but by *living* it in all the moods and actions of life. No matter what you are doing, keep the undercurrent of happiness, the secret river of joy, flowing beneath the sands of various thoughts and the rocky soils of hard trials. Learn to be secretly happy within your heart in spite of all circumstances, and say to yourself, "Happiness is my greatest Divine birthright — the buried treasure of my soul. I have found that at last I shall secretly be rich beyond the dream of kings."

Do not make unhappiness a chronic habit, for it is anything but pleasant to be unhappy, while it is blessedness for yourself and others when you are happy. When it is so easy to wear a silver smile, or to pour sweet happiness through your voice, why be grouchy and scatter unhappiness around you? It is never too late to learn.

Happiness grows by what it is fed on. Learn to be happy by *being* happy all the time.

John said, "If I get money, I shall be happy." He became wealthy. Then he said, "I shall be happy if I get rid of my acute indigestion." His indigestion was cured, but he thought, "If I get a wife, I shall be happy." Then bedlam started, for he married a nagging, tongue-lashing woman. He divorced this wife, and after many years married again, but the second wife was worse than the first one. Then he thought that he would be happier if he divorced his second wife, so he did, but at the age of seventy he thought, "No, I shall never be happy unless I can be youthful again."

In this way people try, but never reach their goal of happiness. They are like the man who raced in anger to bite his own nose, but never could, of course.

Ignorant people, like animals, do not heed the lessons which accompany pain and pleasure. Most people live a life checkered with sadness and sorrow, for they do not avoid the actions which lead to suffering and do not follow the ways which lead to happiness.

Then there are people who are always consciously oversensitive to sorrow and happiness when they come. Such people are usually extremely crushed by sorrow and are overwhelmed by joy, thus losing their mental balance.

There are very few people who, after burning their fingers in the fire of ignorance, learn to avoid misery-making acts.

Many people wish to be happy, and yet they never make the effort to adopt the course of action which leads to happiness. Most people keep rolling down the hill of life only mentally wishing to climb the peak of happiness. They sometimes wake up if their enthusiasm for happiness survives the crash to the bottom of suffering. Most people lack imagination and never wake up until something terrible happens to arouse them from their nightmare of folly.

Stagnant people are unhappy, and extremely ignorant people scarcely know how it feels to be either happy or unhappy. They are unfeeling, like the stones.

It is better to be unhappy about your own ignorance than to die happily with it.

Wherever you are, remain awake and alive with your thought, perception, and intuition, ever ready, like a good photographer, to take pictures of exemplary conduct and to ignore bad behavior. Your highest happiness lies in your being ever ready in desiring to learn and in behaving properly.

People seeking happiness must avoid the influence of bad habits which lead to evil actions, for evil actions produce misery sooner or later. Misery corrodes the body, mind, and soul like a silently burning acid, and cannot be endured long. That is why it should be strictly avoided.

Cure yourself of evil habits by cauterizing them with the opposite good habits. If you have a bad habit of telling lies, and by so doing have lost many friends, start the opposite good habit of telling the truth.

It takes time to form a good habit or a bad one. It is difficult for a bad person to be good and for a good person to be bad; yet, remember that once you become good, it will be natural and easy for you to be good; likewise, if you cultivate an evil habit, you will be compelled to be evil in spite of your desire, and you have to pray, "Father, my spirit is willing, but my flesh is weak."

That is why it is worthwhile to cultivate the habit of being happy.

The man sliding down evil paths finds no resistance; but as soon as he tries to oppose his evil habits by the adoption of spiritual laws of discipline, he finds countless temptations roused to fight and foil his noble efforts.

Your individual happiness depends to a large extent upon protecting yourself and your family from the evil results of gossiping.

See no evil, speak no evil, hear no evil, think no evil, feel no evil.

Most people can talk about other people for hours and thrive under the influence of gossip like the temporary influence of intoxicating poisonous wine. Isn't it strange that people can smoothly, joyously, and with caustic criticism talk about the faults of others for hours, but cannot endure reference to their own faults at all?

If you do not like to talk about your own faults, if it hurts you to do so, you certainly should feel more hurt when saying unkind, harmful things about other people. Train yourself and each member of your family to refrain from talking about others. "Judge not, that ye be not judged."

By giving publicity to a man's weakness, you do not help him. Instead, you either make him wrathful or discouraged, and you shame him, perhaps forever, so that he gives up trying to be good. When you take away the sense of dignity from a person by openly maligning him, you make him desperate.

When a man is down, he is too well aware of his own wickedness. By destructive criticism, you push him still farther down into the mire of despondency into which he is already sinking. Instead of gossiping about him, you should pull him out with loving, encouraging words. Only when aid is asked should spiritual and moral help be offered.

To your own children or loved ones you may offer your friendly, humble suggestions at any time and thus remove their sense of secrecy or delicacy.

Make your home a valley of smiles instead of a vale of tears.

Smile now and never mind how hard it has been for you to do so. Smile *now*. All the time remember to *smile now*, and you will *smile always*.

Some people smile most of the time, while beneath the mask of laughter they hide a sorrow-corroded heart. Such people slowly pine away beneath the shadows of meaningless smiles.

There are other people who smile once in a while, and they may also be very serious at times; yet beneath the hard, beautiful outer appearance there may be gurgling a million fountains of laughing peace.

If you enjoyed good health for fifty years and then were sick for three years, unable to get healed by any method, you would probably forget about the length of time that you enjoyed good health and laughed at the idea of sickness. Now your reaction should be exactly the opposite. Just because you may have been sick for three years is no reason for thinking that you will never be well again.

Likewise, if you were happy a long time, and you have been unhappy a comparatively short time, you are apt to lose hope of ever being happy again. This is lack of imagination. The memory of a long-continued happiness should be a forceful subconscious habit to influence your conscious mind and ward off the consciousness of your present trouble.

When wealth only is lost, nothing real is lost, for if one has health and skill, one can still be happy and can make more money; but if health is lost, then most happiness is also lost, and when the principle of life is lost, all happiness is lost.

After bathing yourself in the ocean of peace in dreamland, as you awake with happiness, say, "In sleep-land I found myself free from mortal worries. I was a king of peace. Now, as I work in the daytime and carry on my diurnal battles of duties, I will no longer be defeated by insurgent worries of the kingdom of wakefulness. I am a king of peace in sleep-land, and I shall continue to be such a king in the land of wakefulness. As I come out of my kingdom of peace in sleep-land, I shall spread that same peace in my land of wakeful dreams."

Being Strong on the Path to Happiness

Happiness is a will-o'-the-wisp which most people follow, and which oftentimes leads them astray until they drown in the marshes of suffering.

Most temporary, easily attained, so-called happiness is nothing but suffering in disguise. It may be pleasant to the palate to eat a great deal at the table, but remember that such procedure is very likely to have many unpleasant after-effects, such as acute indigestion or stomach ache, so also is it with immoderation in your natural impulses. They generally give you sense pleasures in the beginning, but ultimately they produce satiety and unhappiness.

The greatest way to create happiness for yourself is not to allow sense lures or bad habits to control you, but rather be a stern, iron-like ruler of your habits and appetites. Remember that just as you cannot satisfy your own hunger by feeding some other person, so you cannot be really happy by trying to satisfy only the over-demands of your senses.

Too much luxury, instead of producing happiness, drives it away from your mind. Do not spend all your time in finding ways and means which you think will make you happy. Be contented always, equally in your struggle for prosperity, and also in your attainment of it.

You can be a king of happiness in a tattered cottage, or you can be a tortured victim of unhappiness even if you live in a palace. Happiness is mostly a mental phenomenon. You must first establish it firmly within yourself, and then with an undying resolution always to be happy, go through the world seeking health, prosperity, and wisdom.

Remember that to battle failure and sickness and to seek success ever with a happy attitude will bring you far, far nearer to your desired goal than if with an unhappy mind you try to gain your heart's desire, no matter what that desire may be.

Creating Inner Happiness

Happiness depends to some extent upon external conditions, but chiefly upon conditions of the inner mind.

In order to be happy, one must have good health, an efficient mind, a prosperous life, the right work and, above all, an all-round, all-accomplishing wisdom. A man cannot be happy just by holding the inner calm while completely ignoring the struggle for existence and the effort for success. Even Jesus had to eat and clothe himself.

Then again, without internal happiness, one may find oneself a prisoner of worries in a rich castle.

Happiness is not dependent upon success and wealth alone, but real happiness depends upon struggling against the failures, difficulties, and problems of life with an acquired attitude of unshakable internal happiness.

To be unhappy in trying to find the hard-to-acquire happiness defeats its own end. Happiness comes by *being* internally happy first, at all times, while struggling your utmost to uproot the causes of unhappiness.

The habit of preserving an internal happy attitude of mind should have been started when you were very young, but never mind, it is not too late to begin now. From today on, make up your mind that when you meet your trying relatives, when you come in contact with your overbearing office boss, and when you contact your enemies and the trials of life, that you will try to retain your internal calmness and happiness, under all circumstances.

If you persevere in carrying out this resolution in your daily actions and do not forget after a few days of trial, you will find that internal serenity and happiness depend upon a right mental habit and upon resolving to be happy in spite of everything.

But remember, when you learn to be happy at all times, do not allow this independent mental attitude of inner happiness to make you lazy, and do not ignore the material causes which stand in the way of your happiness. Strive to remove them, and go through all the activities of life with this calm, happy attitude of mind.

Putting Funds in Your Happiness-Bank

America is the most prosperous, starving nation on the face of the earth. I never before heard such dollar-begging cries of mentally-poor millionaires even in the streets of Baghdad. It is natural to expect shameless beggars with tattered dress in the streets of the Orient to harass the passer-by with the request for pennies, but it is pitiful to see how mentally-poor rich people sit in the panic-stricken and deserted streets of business crying out about the depression.

The stock market made mentally-rich people, who were satisfied with paper profits. Since the fall of the stock market, they have become mentally poor. The false paper securities made them imagine that they were rich. Now a few strokes of the pen on those same securities makes them think that they are poor. They would do well to write every day in their minds with letters of concentration — that they are rich. It is better to be rich in your thoughts than to believe in melting, fickle securities which make you think that you are rich when you are not.

If you are a person who once believed so much in well-printed, well-signed securities and now are disillusioned, you should try to realize more and more the unchangeable value to yourself of your ability, which you write on the parchment of your determination. Remember that the wealth of *mental* happiness, securely acquired, never can decrease in value, as do stocks and bonds. The latter are controlled by others, whereas you can control your own gold of happiness by your unchanging mental attitude and your resolution "to be happy always."

Your hard-earned money kept for safety in a bank may be lost completely through the failure of that bank, but your well-controlled spiritual happiness, saved in the bank of your staunch, unchangeable determination, never can be lost but will ever increase in value. You are all the officers, the president, and the directors, as well as the investors, in your own happiness-bank; and if you know how to play these various roles, continually creating, preserving, and adding to your happiness deposits, then no failure ever can be possible for you in this, your very own, *bank of happiness.*

Cultivate the Plant of Happiness

D o you ever think seriously of salvaging your treasure of happiness which is sunk beneath the sea of your tumultuous life? Can you make your half-dead rose plant of life bloom again?

We are usually born rich with smiles, youth, strength, beauty, health, mystic aspirations, and swelling, thrilling hopes. As we live and grow, we begin to lose these riches, and the roses in us begin to fade. Why is this? Are we to grow warm with riches and then suddenly be frozen by the chill of poverty? The rose blooms only to die. Does our happiness come only in order to vanish?

No, the rose usually dies on the bed of beauty, yet some roses, worm-eaten, encounter a premature, ugly death. We want to bloom with good actions, fragrant with happiness, and to rest forever with the memories of those who appreciate us. We do not have to die devoured by poverty, sickness, or sorrow.

To guard our rose plant, we must attend to it properly with much digging, watering, feeding, and guarding it from pests and chill.

The rose plant of our happiness can grow only on the abundant, fertile soil of our peace. It can never grow on hard, stony, unfeeling soil of human mentality. We have to constantly dig into peace with the spade of our good actions. We have to keep our happiness plant well-watered with our spirit of love and service. We can only be happy by making others happy.

The real food for the happiness tree can be supplied only through meditation and actual contact with God in daily life. Without our contact with the Infinite source, from which all our human faculties and inspirations spring, we can never grow perfectly and completely.

The worst pests which attack our plant of happiness are lack of the desire to progress, self-satisfaction, and skepticism. The chill of inertia, or lack of definite, constant effort to know the Truth, is the greatest ill from which our happiness plant suffers.

Self-improvement is a Key to Happiness

If you want to be loved, start loving others who need your love.

If you expect others to be honest with you, then start by being honest yourself.

If you do not want others to be wicked, then you must cease to be evil yourself.

If you want others to sympathize with you, start showing sympathy to those around you.

If you want to be respected, you must learn to be respectful to everyone, both young and old.

If you want a display of peace from others, you must be peaceful yourself.

If you want others to be religious, start being spiritual yourself.

Remember, whatever you want others to be, *first be that yourself*; then, you will find others responding in like manner to you.

It is easy to wish that others would behave perfectly toward you, and it is easy to see their faults, but it is very difficult to conduct yourself properly and to consider your own faults. If you can remember to behave rightly, others will try to follow your example. If you can find your own faults without developing an inferiority complex, and can keep busy correcting yourself, then you will be using your time more profitably than if you spent it in just wishing others to be better. Your good example will do more to change others than your wishing, your holy wrath, or your words.

The more you improve yourself, the more you will elevate others around you. The self-improving man is the increasingly happy man. The happier you become, the happier will be the people around you.

The Antidote of Happiness

Remember: No matter how much you are accustomed to being unhappy, you must adopt the antidote of happiness.

Each act of being happy *now* will help you to cultivate the habit of *always* being happy.

Pay no attention if your mind tells you that you can never be happy. Just remember to start being happy now, and every moment, every day, say, "I am happy *now!*"

If you can continuously do that, then, when you look back, you can say, "I have been very happy," and when you look at yourself now you will say, "I am happy," and when you look ahead, you will say, "I know I shall be happy."

Since all of your future happiness depends upon how happy you are now, start being happy *now*.

Be Strong in Your Happiness

Persons of strong character are usually the happiest. They do not blame others for troubles that can usually be traced to their own actions and lack of understanding. They know that no one has any power to add to their happiness or detract from it unless they themselves are so weak that they allow the adverse thoughts and wicked actions of others to affect them.

A strong determination to be happy will help you, but do not wait for your circumstances to change, thinking that there lies the trouble. Try to be happy under *all* circumstances. Do not try to make your happiness conditional to certain desired changes, except in rare cases. If your happiness sometimes seems to depend upon certain circumstances, then, in that case, change your circumstances so that you will be happy instead of sad all the time.

Don't be bound by set rules, as there are exceptions to every rule. Perhaps you say, "If this or that happens, I shall be very contented." Don't wait. Snatch the highest prize of happiness that is within your reach now, for it is the will-o'-the-wisp of hoping for and postponing happiness which leads you to go through many sloughs of disappointment.

Make up your mind that you will be happy whether you are rich or poor, healthy or unhealthy, happily married or unhappily married, old or young, smiling or crying. Don't wait for yourself or your family or your surroundings to change before you can be happy within yourself.

Make up your mind to be happy within yourself, right now, whatever you are, or wherever you are.

Won't-Power Creates Happiness

⸺⸺⸺ ❖ ⸺⸺⸺

If you are a slave to the senses, you cannot be happy. If you are a master of your desires and appetites, you can be a really happy man. If you eat against your will, if you wish anything contrary to your conscience, if you act wrongly, forced by your senses, against the wish of your inner self, then you cannot be happy.

People who are slaves to the senses find that their evil habits compel them to do things which will hurt them. Stubborn bad habits bludgeon your will power down every time it tries to take the lead and guide your thoughts to the kingdom of right action. The remedy lies in rescuing your will power from the imprisoning power of the senses.

Remember, one can lead a horse to a lake, but no one can make him drink unless he wants to. Try to develop "won't" power if you haven't enough will power.

When you are at the dinner table and Mr. Greed lures you to eat more than you should and tries to chloroform your self-control and cast you into the pit of indigestion—watch yourself. After partaking of the right quality and quantity of food, just say to yourself, "I won't eat any more," and get up from your chair at the table and run. When somebody calls, "John, come back and eat some more. Don't forget the delicious apple pie (or strawberry shortcake)," just call back and say, "I won't."

Remember, when thoughts of dishonesty, temptation, or revengefulness come to you, they are the soldiers of the dark misery-making senses. They want to conquer the kingdom of your happiness and keep you prisoner in the dungeon of unhappiness and misery. As soon as the soldiers of wrong thoughts rally together to attack your inner peace, wake up the soul soldiers of light, honesty, self-control, and desire for good things, and wage a furious battle.

Remember, it rests with you whether you want greed, sense-slavery, anger, hatred, revengefulness, worries, or inharmonies to rule your life, or whether you will let the divine soldiers of self-control, calmness, love, forgiveness, peace, and harmony rule your mental kingdom.

Drive away the rebel sense habits which have brought misery to the empire of your peace. Be a king of yourself, letting the soldiers of goodness and good habits rule the kingdom of your mind. Then happiness will reign within you forever.

Kindness Fosters Happiness

Unkind words, ill-spoken words used in a fit of emotion, are like a conflagration which spreads over the forest of friendship and burns up all the green plants of courteous dealings and sympathetic thoughts.

People, drunk with excitement and accustomed to anger-slavery, are very often emotional fire-bugs who, at the slightest provocation, light the matches of wrathful words and set fire to the inner peace of souls.

As forest fires cause millions of dollars of loss to the government, so the emotional fire-bugs, by setting fire to the happiness of millions of intelligent people, cause billions of dollars of loss to creative thinking and also cause great waste of human nerve-energy.

If husbands and wives, instead of target practicing on each other with bullets of wrathful language and discourtesies, would try to entertain each other with the soul-solacing charm of kind words, they would create a new happiness in family life. Unkind behaviour, like eczema, increases by discourteous arguments and disagreements.

In order to be kind, it is not necessary to agree about everything, but if you do disagree, always remain calm and courteous.

It is human weakness to get angry and scold, but it shows divine strength to be able to hold the reins over the wild steeds of your temper and speech. No matter what the provocation may be, behave yourself, and by calm silence, or by genuine kind words, show that your kindness is more powerful than the other person's ugliness, and that before the mellow light of your forgiveness all the gathered hatred of years in your enemies will melt away.

If you are suffering from the indigestion of unkindness or choleric crabbiness, drink the medicine of sweetness.

If you make up your mind to change, start by speaking sincere, kind words to those to whom you have been unjustly harsh. Make yourself attractive by wearing the fine garment of genuine, courteous language.

First, be courteous to your immediate relatives. When you can do that, you will be habitually kind to all people.

Remember, you may not have realized it, but it is true that real family happiness has its foundation on the altar of understanding and kind words.

Unkind words are ruthless murderers of life-long friendships, of the peace of souls, and of the harmony of homes. Banish unkind words from your lips forever and make your home life safe from the invasion of sudden partings and trouble.

Sincere, sweet words are nectar to thirsty souls. They are in demand everywhere. Sweet words create happiness in friends, enemies, societies, churches, business offices, and everywhere. People feel happy when a crabby person is removed from their presence, and they are glad when a sweet-voiced, sincere friend appears.

Concentrating on the Sunny Days of Happiness

When a cloudy day comes, think of the clusters of sunny days that you have had. When the blues come and make you feel that they are going to take a permanent lease on your life, think of the numberless days of happiness which you have previously enjoyed.

Remember, it is ingratitude to the Giver of all gifts to forget the healthy smiles enjoyed for fifty years just because you have been sick for six months. There is no sense in unbalancing your mind and deceiving your judgment by forgetting years of happiness by constantly dwelling upon and taking too seriously the sorrows of a few weeks or a few months.

Be not afraid of this temporary mortal ignorance, for within your soul lies buried the unopened mine of the wisdom of God. Since you are made in His Image, all His wisdom and happiness lie hidden somewhere in the disorganized cellar of your subconsciousness.

To smile when all things are going well is easy and natural, but to smile when all things try to ruin you is difficult, supernatural, admirable, and the harbinger of lasting happiness. Become a smile specialist and a doctor of blues, healing all the sad and weary hearts that you meet by the x-ray of your burning smiles.

When you are sick, do not concentrate upon the length of your suffering, but dream and picture to yourself the fountain of youthful, healthful years that you have already enjoyed. What you have had, you can have again if you try hard enough. To give up is the difficult, miserable way in the long run, but to try hard until you succeed is the easiest way.

Banish sadness with joy; destroy sickening thoughts of failure with the tonic of success consciousness. Polish inharmony with the chisel of harmony. Cauterize worries with indifference. Cast sorrows into the flames of happiness. Shame unkindness by kindness. Humiliate discourtesy by courtesy. Dethrone sick thoughts and place King Vitality on the throne of right living.

Banish restlessness and ignorance from the shores of your mind. Establish the kingdom of silence within and the God of Happiness will enter without prayer, invitation, or coaxing.

Learning to Behave
Creates Happiness

Never can I thank my teacher enough for constantly saying to me, "Learn to behave." I used to resent this extremely, for, like most people, I thought that I was a winged angel and that nobody could say anything to improve me. And when anyone did criticize me, I laughed at him, trying to argue violently as to how wrong he was.

However, as wisdom grew, I found out that I had mental mirrors all around me, and that I could see myself better in others, especially in my Master's unprejudiced mind, than I could see myself in the little mirror of my own hazy understanding. I began to associate with calm minds and to ask them how I looked from their mental perceptions, for I found out that there was a difference between what I thought others thought of me and what others actually thought of me in their inner minds.

It takes a lot of courage to risk a word battle, or other trouble, just for telling people their faults. That is why most people are afraid to criticize you to your face. Most people bite you behind your back and silently criticize you in their own minds.

Your intimate friends do not criticize you openly for fear of offending you; but do not forget, they criticize you inwardly, as you do them. If you want to know what your friends think about you, behave yourself perfectly and keep constantly improving yourself by being unselfish, wise, calm, meditative, fearless, sweet, sincere, courteous, methodical, true to your word, unafraid to be firm, and just, so that your friends will be so overwhelmed by your goodness that they will think, and talk loudly, about what you are. Then you will know, if you want to know.

Learn to make yourself behave, and be happy, and you will influence all the people you meet to be well-behaved and happy.

Shoot Your Smiles

Practice shooting burning smiles at the target of sorrowful hearts. Every time somebody's heart of sorrow is pierced with the bullet of your smile, you have "hit the bull's eye." Every day go on a target practice by shooting smiles into the body of sadness.

Remember, you must kill sorrow at sight. Kill the blues with the blade of wisdom. Open a training school and teach willing students how to be sure shots in shooting smiles into the heart of gloom.

Every time you see sad faces, shoot a buckshot of vitalic-spreading smiles there. As soon as you see a sorrowful heart, shoot into it sympathetic smiles and kind words. The minute you see somebody overcome with clouds of sorrow, disperse the clouds by the heavy, continuous cannonading of your courageous smiles.

When you see the gloom of hopelessness, shoot it at once with hope-awakening smiles. Do not form the habit of sorrowing but form the habit of smiling. Make yourself adamant against taking offense and freely forgive and forget those who offend you. Never get angry yourself. Never allow yourself to become the victim of another's anger. Do your best to overcome difficulties, but smile first, last, and all the time.

There is no better panacea for sorrow, no better-reviving tonic, than smiles. There is no greater power with which to overcome failure than a real smile. There is no better ornament than a genuine smile. There is no beauty greater than the smile of peace and wisdom glowing on your face.

The Relationship Between Money and Happiness

Although it is necessary to make money, it is more necessary to gain happiness; for money is made for happiness and not happiness made for money. Those who concentrate upon making money as their only happiness do not find real satisfaction, for no amount of money can buy happiness if it is lost through systematic wrong actions.

People surrounded with money but unable to use it properly in order to make themselves and others happy, die of happiness thirst. Many people forget that making money is only a means to the goal of happiness. It is as ridiculous to concentrate upon the means and forget the end as it is to keep traveling on a road and forget your destination. It is meaningless to develop the insanity of accumulating money and not use it to make yourself and others happy.

Very many people make the mistake of running after money first instead of first seeking happiness. To try to earn money with a disgruntled, worried mind is not only unsuccessful, but it produces more anxiety and unhappiness. The best way lies in trying to make money after first making sure of happiness. Earning money with a serene and happy attitude leads not only to success but insures happiness also.

Happy people make others happy by their example, for actions speak louder than words.

Eliminating Depression
During Financial Depression

J ust now, when everybody is going about crying "depression" is the time to depress depression. No matter if you have no job, for your own good and for the good of everybody else, *you have no right to be depressed.* If you sit in your own home moaning and sobbing about the depression, you do an injustice to yourself by spending the time paralyzing your mind with sorrow instead of keeping it busy with the creative kind of thinking, which alone can show you a way out of your difficulties.

I can forgive the physically lazy man if his body is weak or if it needs rest, but I cannot so easily forgive the mentally lazy, inwardly fossilized man, for he is too lazy to think. Such individuals usually fear to exercise their brains lest they succeed. It is an injustice to your own progressive powers to keep them crippled by sorrow. Instead of sobbing, you must keep your mind busy with continuous, rapid thinking as to how you can secure work for yourself. You must make the business houses in your city so uncomfortable with your never-silent advertisement of yourself, your creative genius, and your ability to work, that they will be glad to give you a job, if only to make you keep quiet. Then, when you are installed in the position, you must keep it by convincing your employers that you are indispensable to them, and that you can do for them what no one else can.

Darkness, too, flees away before the light. By continually crying "abundance," you will chase away from your mind the thought of depression. If you are suffering materially, do not add more injury to yourself by mentally accepting defeat.

Remember that by wiping away dark depression from within and by placing the light of abundance-consciousness in its place, you can kindle hope in the hearts of your family and your neighbors. In a neighborhood of depressed minds groping in the gloom, you can, by your own cheer, teach them to "buck up," and light their own happiness lamps with the tapers of courage, will power, and creative thinking. Depression, like the Spanish "flu" of 1918, is contagious; it has spread all over the world.

But remember that self-confidence and abundance-consciousness spread faster than the disease of depression ever can do. Just as the sun so quickly spreads over half the globe at one time, so the strength of your joy and abundance-consciousness can spread quickly over the dark territories of your own consciousness as well as over that of your family, your neighbors, your country, and the whole world.

Plain Living and High Thinking

ostering the desire for luxuries is the surest way to increase misery. Do not be the slave of things or possessions. Boil down even your needs. Spend your time in search of lasting happiness or bliss. The unchangeable, immortal soul is hidden behind the screen of your consciousness, on which are painted dark pictures of disease, failure, death, and so forth. Lift the veil of illusive change and be established in your immortal nature. Enthrone your fickle consciousness on the changelessness and calmness within you, which is the throne of God; let your soul manifest bliss night and day.

Happiness can be secured by the exercise of self-control, by cultivating habits of *plain living and high thinking*, and by spending less money, even though earning more. Make an effort to earn more so that you can be the means of helping others to help themselves, for one of the unwritten laws decrees that he who helps others to abundance and happiness always will be helped in return by them, and he will become more and more prosperous and happy. This is a law of happiness which cannot be broken. Is it not better to live simply and frugally and grow rich in reality?

The soul's nature is bliss, a lasting inner state of ever-new, ever-changing joy, which eternally gives joy without changing the one made joyous even when that one passes through the trials of physical suffering or death. Desirelessness is not a negation.

You must attain self-control in order to regain the eternal heritage of all-fulfillment lying within your soul. First, give your soul the opportunity to manifest this state, by meditation, and then, constantly living in this state, do your duty to your body and mind and the world.

You need not give up your ambitions and become negative; on the contrary, let the everlasting joy, which is your real nature, help you to realize all your noble ambitions. Enjoy noble experiences with the joy of God. Perform real duties with divine joy.

You are immortal and are endowed with eternal joy. Never forget this during your play with changeable mortal life. This world is but a stage on which you play your parts under the direction of the Divine Stage Manager. Play them well, whether they are tragic or comic, always remembering that your real nature is eternal bliss and nothing else.

The one thing that will never leave you, once you transcend all unstable mental states, is the joy of your soul.

About the Author

Born in 1893, Paramhansa Yogananda was the first yoga master of India to take up permanent residence in the West.

He arrived in America in 1920 and traveled throughout the country on what he called his "spiritual campaigns." Hundreds of thousands filled the largest halls in major cities to see the yoga master from India. Yogananda continued to lecture and write up to his passing in 1952.

Yogananda's initial impact on Western culture was truly impressive. His lasting spiritual legacy has been even greater. His *Autobiography of a Yogi*, first published in 1946, helped launch a spiritual revolution in the West. Translated into more than fifty languages, it remains a best-selling spiritual classic to this day.

Before embarking on his mission, Yogananda received this admonition from his teacher, Swami Sri Yukteswar: "The West is high in material attainments but lacking in spiritual understanding. It is God's will that you play a role in teaching mankind the value of balancing the material with an inner, spiritual life."

In addition to *Autobiography of a Yogi*, Yogananda's spiritual legacy includes music, poetry, and extensive commentaries on the Bhagavad Gita, the *Rubaiyat* of Omar Khayyam, and the Christian Bible, showing the principles of Self-realization as the unifying truth underlying all true religions. Through his teachings and his Kriya Yoga path millions of people around the world have found a new way to connect personally with God.

His mission, however, was far broader than all this. It was to help usher the whole world into Dwapara Yuga, the new Age of Energy in which we live. "Someday," Swami Kriyananda wrote, "I believe he will be seen as the *avatar* of Dwapara Yuga: the way shower for a new age."

Further Explorations

CRYSTAL CLARITY PUBLISHERS

If you enjoyed this title, Crystal Clarity Publishers invites you to deepen your spiritual life through many additional resources based on the teachings of Paramhansa Yogananda. We offer books, e-books, audiobooks, yoga and meditation videos, and a wide variety of inspirational and relaxation music composed by Swami Kriyananda.

See a listing of books below, visit our secure website for a complete online catalog, or place an order for our products.

crystalclarity.com
clarity@crystalclarity.com

14618 Tyler Foote Road
Nevada City, CA 95959

800.424.1055

ANANDA WORLDWIDE

Crystal Clarity Publishers is the publishing house of Ananda, a worldwide spiritual movement founded by Swami Kriyananda, a direct disciple of Paramhansa Yogananda. Ananda offers resources and support for your spiritual journey through meditation instruction, webinars, online virtual community, email, and chat.

Ananda has more than 150 centers and meditation groups in over 45 countries, offering group guided meditations, classes and teacher training in meditation and yoga, and many other resources.

In addition, Ananda has developed residential communities in the US, Europe, and India. Spiritual communities are places where people live together in a spirit of cooperation and friendship, dedicated to a common goal. Spirituality is practiced in all areas of daily life: at school, at work, and in the home. Many Ananda communities offer internships during which one can stay and experience spiritual community firsthand.

For more information about Ananda communities or meditation groups near you, please visit **ananda.org** or call 530.478.7560.

The Original 1946 Unedited Edition of
Yogananda's Spiritual Masterpiece

AUTOBIOGRAPHY OF A YOGI

Paramhansa Yogananda

Autobiography of a Yogi is one of the world's most acclaimed spiritual classics, with millions of copies sold. Named one of the Best 100 Spiritual Books of the twentieth century, this book helped launch and continues to inspire a spiritual awakening throughout the Western world.

Yogananda was the first yoga master of India whose mission brought him to settle and teach in the West. His firsthand account of his life experiences in India includes childhood revelations, stories of his visits to saints and masters, and long-secret teachings of yoga and Self-realization that he first made available to the Western reader.

This reprint of the original 1946 edition is free from textual changes made after Yogananda's passing in 1952. This updated edition includes bonus materials: the last chapter that Yogananda wrote in 1951, also without posthumous changes, the eulogy Yogananda wrote for Gandhi, and a new foreword and afterword by Swami Kriyananda, one of Yogananda's close, direct disciples.

Also available in Spanish and Hindi from Crystal Clarity Publishers.

The Original Writings of
Paramhansa Yogananda

SCIENTIFIC HEALING AFFIRMATIONS
Paramhansa Yogananda

Yogananda's 1924 classic, reprinted here, is a pioneering work in the fields of self-healing and self-transformation. He explains that words are crystallized thoughts and have life-changing power when spoken with conviction, concentration, willpower, and feeling. Yogananda offers far more than mere suggestions for achieving positive attitudes. He shows how to impregnate words with spiritual force to shift habitual thought patterns of the mind and create a new personal reality.

Added to this text are over fifty of Yogananda's well-loved "Short Affirmations," taken from issues of *East-West* and *Inner Culture* magazines from 1932 to 1942. This little book will be a treasured companion on the road to realizing your highest, divine potential.

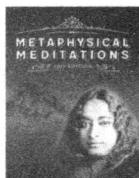

METAPHYSICAL MEDITATIONS
Paramhansa Yogananda

Metaphysical Meditations is a classic collection of meditation techniques, visualizations, affirmations, and prayers from the great yoga master, Paramhansa Yogananda. The meditations given are of three types: those spoken to the individual consciousness, prayers or demands addressed to God, and affirmations that bring us closer to the Divine.

Select a passage that meets your specific need and speak each word slowly and purposefully until you become absorbed in its inner meaning. At the bedside, by the meditation seat, or while traveling — one can choose no better companion than *Metaphysical Meditations*.

SONGS OF THE SOUL
Paramhansa Yogananda

Yogananda preferred to express his wisdom not in dry intellectual terms but as pure, expansive feeling. To drink his poetry is to be drawn into the web of his boundless, childlike love. In one moment his *Songs of the Soul* invite us to join him as he plays among the stars with his Cosmic Beloved. Then they call us to discover that portion of our own hearts that is eternally one with the Nearest and Dearest. This volume is a bubbling, singing wellspring of spiritual healing that we can bring with us everywhere.

The Wisdom of Yogananda *series*

Paramhansa Yogananda's timeless wisdom is offered here in an approachable, easy-to-read format. The writings of the Master are presented with minimal editing to capture his expansive and compassionate wisdom, his sense of fun, and his practical spiritual guidance.

CONVERSATIONS WITH YOGANANDA
Stories, Sayings, and Wisdom of Paramhansa
    Yogananda
*Recorded with reflections, by his disciple, Swami
    Kriyananda*

For those who enjoyed Paramhansa Yogananda's autobiography and long for more, this collection of conversations offers rare intimate glimpses of life with the Master as never before shared.

This is an unparalleled account of Yogananda and his teachings written by one of his foremost disciples. Swami Kriyananda was often present when Yogananda spoke privately with other close disciples, received visitors and answered their questions, and dictated and discussed his writings. He recorded the Master's words, preserving a treasure trove of wisdom that would otherwise have been lost.

These *Conversations* include not only Yogananda's words as he spoke them, but the added insight of a disciple who spent over fifty years attuning his consciousness to that of his guru.

The collection features nearly five hundred stories, sayings, and insights from the twentieth century's most famous master of yoga, as well as twenty-five photos—nearly all previously unreleased.

THE ESSENCE OF SELF-REALIZATION
The Wisdom of Paramhansa Yogananda
Recorded, compiled, and edited by his disciple,
Swami Kriyananda

Filled with lessons, stories, and jewels of wisdom that Paramhansa Yogananda shared only with his closest disciples, this volume is an invaluable guide to the spiritual life, carefully organized in twenty main topics.

Great teachers work through their students, and Yogananda was no exception. Swami Kriyananda comments, "After I'd been with him a year and a half, he began urging me to write down the things he was saying during informal conversations." Many of the three hundred sayings presented here are available nowhere else. This book and *Conversations with Yogananda* are must-reads for anyone wishing to know more about Yogananda's teachings and to absorb his wisdom.

www.ingramcontent.com/pod-product-compliance
Lightning Source LLC
Chambersburg PA
CBHW040122070426
42448CB00043B/3480